A Life for Israel

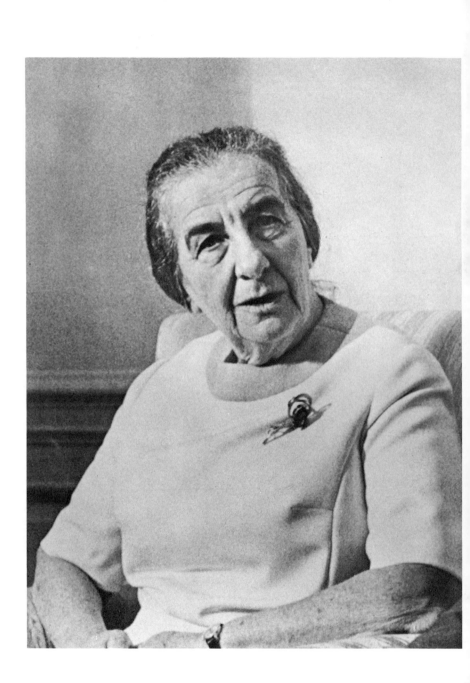

A Life for Israel
The Story of Golda Meir

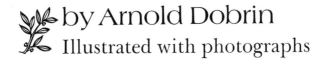 by Arnold Dobrin
Illustrated with photographs

THE DIAL PRESS / NEW YORK

Library of Congress Cataloging in Publication Data
Dobrin, Arnold. A life for Israel.
Bibliography: p.   1. Meir, Golda Mabovitz,
1898–   —Juvenile literature. [1. Meir, Golda
Mabovitz, 1898–   2. Israel—History] I. Title.
DS126.6.M42D6   956.94′05′0924 [B] [92]   73–15442
ISBN 0-8037-6187-2   ISBN 0-8037-6188-0 (lib. bdg.)

For Ande and Brian

Preface

The story of Israel and of Golda Meir, my sister, are closely entwined. Arnold Dobrin has told this moving and dramatic story with sensitivity, perception and deep feeling for the Jewish people. *A Life for Israel* is a fine portrait of Golda. I am sure it will give young readers everywhere a better understanding of how and why Israel came into existence and the devotion, selflessness, and courage which has made its existence possible.

Clara Stern

I want to express my grateful acknowledgment to Mrs. Clara Stern for her thoughtful criticism of my manuscript and for her generous loan of precious family photographs; and to Peggy Mann, Josephine Hansen, Alicia Seyton, Miss Zapinsky of the Zionist Archives in New York, the librarians of the Westport Public Library, the Pioneer Women, the Consulate of Israel, and the Israel Government Information Service in Jerusalem. My thanks, also, to my editor, Regina Hayes, for her patient cooperation, guidance, and encouragement.

Contents

A Life for Israel

The Cossacks Are Coming

Five-year-old Golda ran crying into the house. Her heart was beating fast and her eyes were wide with fear.

"What is it, Golda?" her mother asked with alarm. "Come and tell me what has happened."

Between sobs Golda explained, "I was playing in the lane when the Cossacks came. They were riding so fast I couldn't run away in time. They laughed and made their horses jump over my head. I was so afraid."

Mrs. Mabowitz held her trembling daughter close and comforted her. Stroking her head gently, she said, "The Cossacks are gone, darling. They can't hurt you now."

"Why didn't the Cossacks come to Kiev when we lived there?" Golda asked.

"Because so few Jews lived there," Mrs. Mabowitz explained. "Here in Pinsk there are many thousands of Jewish people. That's why the Cossacks come."

The Cossacks were fierce soldiers in the Russian army. Riding into towns where Jewish people lived, they burned homes, destroyed possessions, and killed men, women, and children. These tragic attacks, carried out with the approval of the government, were called *pogroms*—a word that inspired fear among Russian Jews. Whenever Golda saw neighbors boarding up the windows of their houses, she grew afraid. She knew that they expected a pogrom.

There were other reasons that life for Jews in Russia was hard. Most of the Jewish people had been forced to live in poor, small villages. They were not allowed to travel or live in cities without special permission. Golda's father had been given permission to live in Kiev because he was a skilled carpenter. It was in this city that Golda was born on May 3, 1898.

4

Golda's mother started cooking dinner. For herself there was black bread, potatoes, and a small piece of fish. But the children were having a special treat—porridge. Mrs. Mabowitz hoped that this would help Golda forget what had happened earlier in the lane.

Besides Golda, the Mabowitzes had an older daughter named Shana and an adored baby, Clara. Five other children had been born to Golda's parents but all had died when they were still very young.

Mrs. Mabowitz tried not to think about these tragedies. She kept busy taking care of her three daughters. Now, as she prepared the porridge for supper, she sang a song and tried to be cheerful. But every time she thought of the Cossacks she was sick with fear.

"Come, girls!" she called when the porridge was ready. She set the steaming bowls on the table. Clara, Golda, and Shana ate the delicious food eagerly. But Shana, who was fifteen years old, was still hungry. "Please, Mama," she asked, "can I have some more porridge?"

Mrs. Mabowitz shook her head sadly as she reached for the bread knife. "No," she said. "There is no more porridge. Eat more bread and you will not be hungry."

As soon as she finished supper, Shana helped her mother clean up. She swept the floor and dried the dishes quickly because she was impatient to see her friends. They were young people such as herself who hated the lack of freedom in Russia.

They talked about ways of changing the government. Often they discussed the future and what they could do to make it better. Although they argued about many things, there was one subject on which they all agreed. They were convinced that a national homeland *must* be created for Jewish people in Palestine.

These young people were called Zionists. They belonged to the Zionist organization, which was founded in 1897 by Theodore Herzl, an Austrian writer. Herzl had studied the long history of the Jews carefully and sought a solution for their suffering.

For centuries the Jews had wandered the earth as a homeless, oppressed people. They never gave up the hope of returning to Palestine—the land that had once been theirs. The first Israelite tribes had settled in Palestine twelve centuries before the birth of Christ. In the Bible, God had promised Palestine to the first Hebrew, Abraham. "And I will give to thee, and to thy seed after thee . . . all the land of Canaan, for an everlasting possession (Genesis 12:7)." But invaders came and after the Roman armies destroyed Jerusalem in A.D. 70, the Jewish people were forced to scatter throughout the world. After the Romans

*Theodore Herzl (center), founder of
the Zionist movement*

many conquerers came, including the Ottoman Turks, who gained control of Palestine in 1516 and still ruled at the beginning of this century.

The Zionists believed that the Jews must return to Palestine and rebuild their nation. When Shana studied Herzl's writings, she became an enthusiastic supporter of the Zionists' goals. She longed to join them in their important work. When she talked to her mother and father about Zionism and what she hoped to do, Golda listened carefully.

Before long, certain things became clear to Golda. She began to understand that in Palestine the Jews would no longer be afraid of the Cossacks. In Palestine, where they could live and work as they liked, there would be enough food to eat. In Palestine, Jewish children would not tremble whenever they saw their fathers boarding up the windows of the house.

America! America!

Palestine was not the only country where Russian Jews hoped to go. At the turn of the century large numbers of Jewish people emigrated to America. Some were so happy to be in a land of freedom they kissed the ground when they arrived. In America people could worship God as they pleased and live wherever they wished. Usually they could make enough money to support a family.

Golda's father considered emigrating to Palestine

and then rejected this alternative. He was not a Zionist and did not share his daughter's dream of a Jewish homeland. Having known poverty for many years, he now wanted a chance to improve his family's standard of living.

Finally, in 1903, Mr. Mabowitz decided that he too wanted to try his luck in America. As soon as he had the money he would send for his wife and daughters. They cried when he left and counted the days until his first letter arrived.

Now Mrs. Mabowitz had to be both a mother and a father to her children. Clara was still a baby who needed a lot of attention. Golda, although a little girl, tried to help her mother. Shana, as the eldest, had many duties around the house. Yet every night she left the house as soon as possible. To her any other work or responsibility seemed small compared to the Zionist cause.

Sometimes when she and her friends talked late into the night, her mother grew frantic with worry. "Don't you know that the secret police are everywhere!" she scolded her daughter. "If they catch you they will send you to Siberia!"

People who hoped to change the Russian form of government were often sent to jails in Siberia. Sometimes ten or twenty years passed before prisoners

*A rare photograph of the Mabowitz family
shows Golda, Shana, and Clara (left to right)
standing behind their parents.*

were released. Shana knew of this danger but she was willing to risk it for a cause that was so important.

"That's a chance I will have to take," Shana told her mother. "We *must* work for a better life and to have our own country some day. Otherwise our lives will be miserable."

"*Please* be careful," begged Mrs. Mabowitz.

"I'll try," answered Shana, "but I won't stop meeting my friends. Our work is more important than anything else!"

Mrs. Mabowitz could not stop worrying about her daughter. She knew that young Golda was listening carefully when Shana's friends met at the Mabowitz house. She was afraid that the entire family would suffer if Shana was discovered.

Finally she decided that there was only one thing to do. She must not wait for her husband to send for them. Instead, she must take her children to America as quickly as possible. At once Mrs. Mabowitz began to sell her possessions to raise money for the journey.

Shana did not want to leave her friends, but Golda was excited by the idea of going to the distant land called America. Her father was living in a town with the strange name of Milwaukee. What a curious word! Golda said it again and again, "Milwaukee . . . Milwaukee . . ." as she tried to imagine what it was like.

"Is it very far away?" she asked her mother.

"Yes, *very* far," Mrs. Mabowitz said.

To get there was a long and tiring journey. First Mrs. Mabowitz and her daughters took a train to Antwerp in Belgium. Here they waited five days for the ship that would take them across the Atlantic Ocean. The trip took many weeks, but even after they arrived in Quebec, still another long journey awaited them.

Golda thought they would *never* get to the place called Milwaukee. But finally, well over a month after they had left Russia, that exciting day came. Looking out the train window, Golda saw a man hurrying along the platform. He was eagerly looking into each window he passed.

Suddenly, Golda's mother saw him. "There!" she called excitedly. *"There he is!* Your father has come for us!"

Runaway

Golda ran to her father as soon as she could get off the train. He held her high in his arms and then kissed her as he hugged her tight. "How my little Golda has grown!" he said laughing happily. Then he embraced his other children and his wife. Soon the family was sitting around a table where they talked about the many things that had happened since Mr. Mabowitz's arrival in America.

"This is a wonderful country," he said. "But it is

not easy to make money even in America. I have not been able to find an apartment I can afford."

"Certainly there must be some place for us to live," said Golda's mother.

"Yesterday I found some rooms in the back of a store," said Mr. Mabowitz. "But if we take the rooms we must take the store as well."

"Then we will take it!" said Golda's mother. "I have always wanted to have a little store. Now I will have the chance to do it!"

Soon the Mabowitz family moved into the tiny apartment behind the store. Mr. Mabowitz got a job as a carpenter with the railroad and Mrs. Mabowitz was kept busy selling groceries. Neither of the girls liked to work in the store but their mother insisted. She needed someone to stay there while she went downtown for new supplies. Golda dreaded having to work in the mornings because then she would be late for school. This not only embarrassed her very much but she was also sorry to miss some of the morning lessons.

"Please, Mother," she asked. "Can't you close the store until you get back from town? I don't want to be late to school again."

"No," Mrs. Mabowitz explained. "We can't disappoint our customers."

*In an eighth-grade class photograph, Golda is
at far right, wearing a white dress.*

"*Please,* Mother!" Golda begged as she felt tears forming in her eyes. "I just hate being late."

"You *must* stay in the store," Mrs. Mabowitz said firmly. "The customers need food. We need money. *Now I don't want to hear another word about it!*" And off she went to buy more supplies at the wholesale market.

Shana too had problems with her mother. She did not want to work at the store and she did not want to marry a man chosen by her parents. Her arguments with her mother were far worse than Golda's. Her interest in Zionism was as strong as ever. She often spent her free time with other Zionists and tried to interest more people in the movement.

Now that Shana was over eighteen and could do as she wished, she decided to move out of her parents' home and get a job. After working in Milwaukee for a time she went to Denver. Before long she married a young man, also a Zionist, whom she had known in Russia.

Her parents were so bitterly angry and hurt that they refused to write to Shana. But Golda secretly wrote to her older sister. Shana sent her letters to a neighbor, who gave them to Golda when she came to visit. Golda could tell that her sister was much happier away from home. She wished she too could have the same freedom.

Golda was now a young teen-ager. She was outgoing, popular, ambitious, and sure of what she wanted. Her friends saw that she was intensely idealistic. Golda could never be satisfied unless she was working for a cause. But more and more she was finding out that her goals differed widely from those of her parents.

The Mabowitzes wanted their daughters to be happy, but they continued to cling to the strict customs of the Old World. It was difficult for them to understand that Golda was a strong-minded girl with ideas of her own. Her opportunities here in America were different from what they had been in Russia. Now Golda began to argue with her mother and father just as Shana had.

The worst arguments grew out of discussions about Golda's future. She was a good student who made excellent grades. Proudly showing her report card to her parents, she said, "When I finish high school, I'm going to go to the teacher's training school."

"And what will you do there?" asked her father.

"I will learn to be a teacher, of course," Golda answered.

"Oh, no you won't, my dear child!" said Mr. Mabowitz. "If you must go to school, go to a commercial school. There you can learn to be a good secretary. Girls do not need any other education. They need only to marry a nice young man and settle down!"

"Marriage can come later," Golda said. "Now I want to be a teacher."

"But you just can't!" Golda's mother scolded. "Young men don't like girls who are too intelligent."

Golda refused to listen to her parents. She would never change her mind about continuing her education. As she became more determined, her arguments with her parents grew worse and worse. Finally, when she was only fourteen, Golda realized she could no longer stay in her parents' house.

Writing to Shana in Denver, she said that she could not stand the continual fights with her parents. She begged Shana to let her come and live in Denver. By return mail she received a letter telling her to come at once. Enclosed was money for a railway ticket. That day Golda began her plans to run away from home. She went next door to tell her friend Regina what she intended to do.

"Will you keep a bundle of clothes for me?" she asked her friend.

"Of course," Regina said. "But why do you want me to do that?"

"So that when I leave the house in the morning, no one will suspect what I am going to do. I'll pick the clothes up at your house and go to the station. By evening I will be on my way to Denver."

Regina wasn't sure that Golda was doing the right thing. Golda wasn't either. But she knew that she and her parents could no longer endure the terrible fights they were having. Perhaps it would be better for everyone if Golda went away for a while.

The next morning Golda kissed her mother and father good-bye as usual. But instead of going to school, she went next door to get her clothes. Soon she was at the railway station, frightened and happy at the same time. She knew only one thing for certain: she *had* to go.

The following evening, Golda and Shana were happily talking about the subjects that were so important to them. Golda gave her sister news of their parents. Then Golda asked if there were many Zionists in Denver and answered Shana's questions about her Zionist friends in Milwaukee.

The following days were busy. Golda attended high school in the daytime and helped Shana with the housework in the late afternoon. At night Shana and her husband frequently had guests at their house. Many of these young people were Zionists, but there was one young man who was more interested in music than in politics. He was a dark-haired young fellow named Morris Myerson. Morris was gentle, intelligent, and had a great love for the arts. He and Golda went to many concerts together. He also introduced Golda to the romantic poetry he enjoyed so much. Soon he and Golda were seeing each other very often.

Six months later Golda was so fond of Morris she found it difficult to say good-bye to him. But the time had come to leave Denver. Golda's parents had written to her, begging that she return home. They promised that she could become a teacher if she still wanted to.

Golda knew that her parents missed her very much. And she wanted to see them again. She had learned a lot by leaving home, but she knew also that it would be good to return home again.

Waiting, Hoping, Working

Golda enrolled at the Milwaukee Normal School for the teacher training course in 1916. She enjoyed the courses as much as she knew she would and she looked forward to the day when she would have her own class. And yet, although she would have been a good teacher, it is doubtful that Golda would have been satisfied with teaching. Her dedication to Zionism was too strong. Golda's outstanding trait was her idealism, her need to give her life to the larger goals she set for herself. She was an activist—a person who had a great need to do, to build, to organize.

During these years she did not realize how important such needs were to her. Studies took most of her time and, as before, she continued to get excellent grades. Still, there were times when she wanted fun and pleasure.

Morris Myerson had followed Golda to Milwaukee and they continued to spend a great deal of time together. They enjoyed concerts and picnics and often read poetry aloud. Frequently they discussed the sad and disturbing news from Europe.

World War I had begun in 1914. The people of Europe suffered terribly as German armies devastated one country after another. In Poland and Russia many Jews were shot. Other Jews were beaten and their possessions destroyed.

Golda knew that these people needed as much help as they could get. Money must be raised to buy food, clothing, and shelter. But these were only short-term goals that would help keep these people alive. The great problem the Jews had faced for so many centuries still remained: they *must* have a homeland of their own. But where could this be created?

Some people suggested that the Jews be given their own country in Africa. Others said they should have a part of Australia. But the great majority of the Jewish people felt that only *one* country could become the homeland—Palestine.

Golda believed in this solution, suggested years before by Theodore Herzl. At first only a small group of intellectuals had joined Herzl's Zionist movement. Later, Zionism spread throughout the world as Jews everywhere realized they must work to make the homeland a reality. For only then could they live as equals with other men and women in the world. Only then would they be given the same respect other people are given.

Already there were groups of Jews in Palestine working to build up the country. Golda yearned to be there with them. The time was coming close when she would have to make a decision about her future.

What should she do? She loved America. Without the freedom and opportunity it offered, her family would still be living the same sad, poor lives in Russia. How could she plan to leave America and move thousands of miles away when she and Morris were planning to be married soon? But how could she enjoy her freedom when she knew that millions of other Jews had none at all?

At last she made her decision. She would go to Palestine. There she would help build the nation she had dreamed of. Someday, thousands of Jews would be coming to the new land. Much work must be done to prepare for that day. Farms had to be cultivated in the desert soil. Orchards had to be planted and new industries constructed. To accomplish all this would be an enormous task.

When Shana heard that Golda was going to Palestine, she decided to join her. Shana's husband had to continue working in the United States for the time being so he could support his wife and the children who had recently been born to them. He planned to join his family when they were settled. Clara, who was attending the University of Wisconsin, planned to follow them as soon as she finished her studies.

Now the hardest part remained—the time had come when Golda must tell Morris about her plan. When she finished he shook his head sadly. "But Golda," he protested, "you know I don't feel the same way that you do about Palestine. I hoped we would live in America after we were married. This is a good country and I want to bring up our family here."

"Of course America is a good country," Golda said. "But there will never be a Jewish homeland unless we work for it."

"It will be a long time yet before there is a homeland," Morris said.

"Perhaps," Golda agreed. "But the time will come closer if we work hard now." She hated terribly to go on but she knew she must be completely honest with Morris. "If you will come and work with me in Palestine we can still be married. If you won't come, I can't marry you—even though I love you."

Finally Morris agreed and he and Golda were married in a Milwaukee synagogue. They promised each other in the marriage vows that they would both go to Palestine. Golda would have liked to leave at once but the war was still going on. Instead, she contented herself with organizing new Zionist groups and raising money. For this work she was paid only fifteen dollars a week. Golda didn't mind, because it was the work that was important to her, not the money.

Everywhere she went she explained Zionist aims and asked for contributions. She also asked that young men and women plan to go to Palestine when the war was over.

Her goal—and that of Zionists everywhere—took a tremendous leap forward on November 17, 1917. It was on this day that the British government, then in control of Palestine, issued the Balfour Declaration. It stated that the government supported the creation of a Jewish state in Palestine.

A family portrait: Shana, her husband and children are in the foreground, Morris Myerson and Golda behind.

But the British intended to move slowly. During World War I the Turks had fought with the Germans against the Allies, the name given to the combined armies of Britain, France, and the United States. The peace treaty signed at the end of the war forced the defeated Turks to surrender Palestine to Great Britain. It gave the British a mandate—the power to establish a government—for an indefinite time. Great Britain used this power to maintain her influence in the Middle East and was reluctant to give it up.

And yet the announcement of the Balfour Declaration was of the greatest importance: it declared that for the first time in history a major European country agreed to the establishment of a Jewish nation.

The British government issued the Balfour Declaration partly because of its sense of obligation to one man—Chaim Weizmann. Weizmann was a Jewish scientist who worked in England during World War I. Because of his discoveries the British were able to make superior explosives.

Golda revered Chaim Weizmann as a great scientist and a great Zionist. As she thought of all that his work and the work of other Zionists had accomplished, a great wave of joy and thankfulness overcame her. At last the goal they had worked for was a little closer.

Waiting, Hoping, Working

The time to go to Palestine had finally come. Golda found there were a thousand things to do before they could leave. But now her impatience to be off grew stronger with each passing day. She didn't want to waste a minute.

Kibbutz in the Desert

One of the things that attracted Golda to Palestine was the chance to join a *kibbutz*. This Hebrew word meaning "group" or "gathering" is used to describe a communal farm. The people who join a kibbutz agree to work for the good of the entire group. Each person contributes his labor or any other special abilities he or she has, and each person receives whatever is needed from the group.

Within the kibbutz no one is allowed to use money.

And everything in the kibbutz—the land, cattle, houses, and equipment—belongs to the group. People who join the kibbutz are called *kibbutzniks*.

Most of the early kibbutzniks were intellectuals. They were eager to contribute to the communal life of the kibbutz. They also saw it as a very practical way of living in Palestine with its dangers and hardships. A kibbutz could be defended more easily than an isolated farmhouse. It also provided a livelihood for immigrants who had absolutely no money or possessions.

In the kibbutz, women were expected to do the same jobs as the men. Nurseries were provided for the care of the children, who visited their parents when the day's work was over.

Golda and Morris applied to a kibbutz called Merhavia. One of the first kibbutzim in Palestine, Merhavia was founded by a small band of young men and women from Russia. At first the kibbutzniks did not want to accept Golda and her husband. Golda could not understand why. Finally, one of her friends, who was a member of the kibbutz, told her the reason.

"You are an American girl," she explained. "You are used to a much easier life than we have here. The kibbutzniks think you will not be able to do the hard labor that is necessary. And the toilets and showers are far from the place where you will sleep."

"I may be an American," Golda said, "but I can work as hard as they can!"

"But our lives at Merhavia are *very* hard," Golda's friend warned her again. "It is very different from America. Are you *sure* you know what you are getting into?"

"Yes. Absolutely, completely sure!" Golda said firmly. "More than anything else in the world I want to be a kibbutznik!"

At last, toward the end of 1921, Golda and her husband were accepted at Merhavia. Then Golda had the chance to prove that she meant what she said. Much of the work of the kibbutzniks was planting citrus fruit trees. The semiarid climate of Palestine was ideal for growing oranges, lemons, and grapefruit, and the kibbutzniks hoped that one day fruit growing would become an important industry throughout the land.

Because the ground was rocky the soil first had to be loosened with picks. This was hard work even for someone who was accustomed to heavy labor. But Golda worked with the pick every day. In the evening when she returned to her room, she was so tired she could hardly move a finger.

"Just rest here," her husband said. "I'll bring you some food from the kitchen."

(*Above*) *Merhavia in the early years;*
(*below*) *Golda at work in the fields at Merhavia*

"No you won't!" Golda said. "You're just as tired as I am. Besides, everyone would say, 'What did I tell you? That's an American girl for you!' "

"*Please*, Golda," Morris pleaded. "You're so tired you can't even keep your eyes open."

"Yes, that's true," Golda agreed. "But somehow I'll find a way to eat dinner with the others." Although every bone in her body ached, Golda joined the other young men and women in the dining room.

Soon it was Golda's turn to be the kibbutz cook. She was glad for this opportunity because the food at Merhavia was very bad. One of the main dishes was chick-peas cooked in bitter oil—the only oil the kibbutzniks could afford to buy. There were also a few vegetables from the small vegetable garden. Sometimes the kibbutzniks were given canned beef left by the British army.

The worst part of the kibbutz food was the canned herrings that were served for breakfast. Golda bought oatmeal and served steaming bowls of it every morning. Although it tasted good and was cheap, the other women in the kibbutz were furious. "Golda is ruining the kibbutzniks!" they complained. "She is coddling them and soon they will want to have their herrings skinned and boned before they eat them!"

Golda answered, "What would you do in your own

home? You would not serve your own family herrings for breakfast. *This* is your home! The kibbutzniks are *your* family."

Golda had many other jobs besides planting trees and cooking. She picked almonds, managed the chicken houses, and also worked in the barley fields planting and harvesting.

In the summer, great hordes of flies came to the fields. To protect herself, Golda wore a dress with a high collar and long sleeves. She wrapped her head in a scarf and spread Vaseline on her face. Since the flies were not so bad in the darkness, Golda got up at four in the morning to work.

She said that the flies were the worst problem at the kibbutz. Even the cows would stampede in the fields when the flies became active. "I had a solution for all my other problems," Golda said, "but not for the flies."

And yet there was still another problem which Golda could not solve. Morris insisted that they leave Merhavia. Golda insisted just as strongly that they stay.

Morris had never been as physically strong as Golda. Although he always tried to do the same work as the other kibbutzniks, it strained his endurance. When he had an attack of malaria he became very ill and was taken to a hospital. Returning to Merhavia in a weakened state, he could not work for a long time. It seemed that he would never be strong enough for life on a kibbutz.

One day he said to Golda, "I've tried this life just as I promised I would. But it's not for me. I don't like manual labor. I don't like living with so many people. And some day when we have children, I don't want them to be brought up in a kibbutz nursery!"

"You know I love Merhavia," Golda flashed back. "And you know how hard we have worked here. Why should we leave now just when the kibbutz is growing so fast?"

"Because I believe it is not for us," Morris argued. "We've lived the way you want to for a long time. Now it is only fair that we try to live as I think we should. I miss hearing music. I miss going to art exhibitions. I want to live in a city again."

Golda realized that unless she agreed to leave the kibbutz her marriage would be finished. It was a painful decision for her to make. Life at Merhavia was just as hard as Golda had been warned that it was. But she was never sorry that she and Morris had gone there to live and work. She told people these years were the happiest of her life. "There's nothing I've loved so much as kibbutz life," she explained. "I've liked everything in it—the manual work, the comradeship, the discomforts."

As they packed to leave, Morris sang happily for the first time in years. But leaving was a bitter time for Golda.

Marriage Is Not Enough

Soon Golda had little time to regret her departure from Merhavia. In 1924 she gave birth to a son, Menahem. Two years later her daughter Sarah was born. It was not easy for her to care for two babies in their tiny apartment in Tel Aviv. Two small rooms— a crowded, uncomfortable apartment—was all that Golda and Morris could afford.

There was no gas or electricity so kerosene lamps were used for light. Golda did the cooking in a tin shack in the backyard. They had enough money to buy a bed but not much more. For tables and bookcases they used orange crates.

But even these economies did not help enough. Finally Golda had to go to work for a few hours every day. She taught English at a private school and also took in laundry. The latter was very hard because she had to heat each pail of water that she used.

Golda had worked hard before. She had been poor. But in the past she had been able to work toward her goal—the Jewish national homeland. Now she was so busy being a wife and mother that she did not have time to do anything else. Golda believed that it is important to be a good wife. She knew too that being a good mother is one of the most important jobs in the world. But she also realized that for some women, marriage is not enough. Golda grew more and more dissatisfied.

Morris often noticed the faraway expression on her face. He was worried about the unhappy atmosphere that filled the apartment. One day he said, "Tell me what's wrong, Golda. Why do you always look so miserable when I come home from work? I know that you love our children. Why should you be so unhappy?"

"Yes, of course I love the children," Golda agreed. "But I can't be content with cooking and cleaning and looking after babies. I don't mind the hard work, but I have a brain too. I want to use it. And I have an ideal. I came to Palestine to help build a new country. But I can't do that while I'm washing the children and doing the housework."

"What is it you want?" Morris asked. "You are already teaching English."

"I want a full-time job, a job where I can contribute something," Golda said. "There are so many things that need to be done here."

"But who will take care of the children?" Morris asked.

"The woman who comes in now for a few hours while I'm gone will probably work full time. If not, I'll find someone else. We can pay her salary out of the money that I'll get at my new job."

"I don't like the idea," Morris said sadly, "but if that is the only thing that will make you happy, you must do it."

Golda soon found a job with the Women's Labor Council, where she was able to use her abilities to the fullest extent. She planned new farms where immigrant girls could learn about farm life. She helped develop kindergartens where working women could leave their children. Golda had always been skilled at organization. Now, as she used this skill, it grew even stronger.

Later Golda moved on to new jobs. Each job brought more responsibility. People had begun to notice that Golda had great leadership ability. She could be tough when necessary but she knew the value of a gentle word. Such instinctive knowledge she put to work in directing the people who worked for her.

And, as always, work took an enormous amount of her time. She had little energy left for her children—until 1932, when a serious problem demanded all her attention. Golda's daughter Sarah was dangerously ill with a kidney disease she had suffered from since birth. None of the doctors in Palestine could help her. They said there was very little hope she could survive.

Golda refused to accept their views. She had read that doctors in New York City were having success with patients who suffered from the same disease as Sarah. If only Golda could take Sarah to New York. She thought about the problem for several days and then made her decision.

Golda went to the directors of the Women's Labor Council. She told them her problem and asked for an assignment that would take her to America. She said that if she did not take her daughter to New York, there was a good chance Sarah would die.

Golda was assigned to work with a women's group in New York called The Pioneers. The members of this group wanted to interest large numbers of American women in the Zionist cause. They needed a dynamic speaker who was devoted to Zionism and well acquainted with its work in Palestine. No other woman could do the job as well as Golda. From her earliest teens she had helped to raise money—another important goal of the Pioneer women.

Sarah was put into a hospital as soon as she, her mother, and Menahem arrived in New York. Golda had many responsibilities because Morris had remained in Palestine to work. After Sarah was settled, Golda asked an old friend who lived in Brooklyn to look after Menahem. He was enrolled in school there but had difficulty adjusting to it. He was lonely and wanted to return to Israel. Golda comforted him as best she could but she had to travel a great deal to carry out her work and could not stay with him for long.

At last Menahem found some consolation in a new-found musical talent. One day he heard the beautiful sound of a cello—an instrument with which he was unfamiliar. Its sound fascinated him so much he decided that someday he too would become a cellist. Menahem began lessons as soon as Golda could afford to buy him a cello.

Golda visited Sarah at the Beth Israel Hospital whenever she could. Before long, she was told that Sarah was responding to treatment and would recover completely. Golda was overjoyed. Relieved of this worry, she could now plunge into her work. She could raise the money so desperately needed in Palestine.

After two years in America, Golda and the children returned to Palestine. There Golda could see the many ways the money she had raised was being spent. The funds had made it possible to build schools and hospitals, to buy farm equipment, and to construct factories. But now more and more money was needed to buy guns and ammunition.

In 1933 Adolf Hitler had come to power in Germany. His government, which was strongly anti-Jewish, passed laws that prevented Jews from attending school. They could not own land or businesses. Their temples were burned. As life in Germany became impossible—and showed every indication of becoming worse—thousands of German Jews came to Palestine.

When the Arabs saw the Jewish population growing, they became alarmed. Propaganda spread by wealthy Arab landowners warned that the Jews would

take over all the land and push out the Arabs. Soon
roving bands began to kill Jews and to burn Jewish
homes and businesses. They were determined to stop
the flow of Jews to Palestine.

Before long the kibbutzniks were digging trenches.
They stretched barbed wire around the kibbutzim
and armed themselves. An underground army called
the Haganah was created. It rushed to help defend
Jewish communities wherever the need arose.

Golda became one of the leaders of the Haganah.
She also wrote for a secret radio station called The
Voice of Israel. But most of her energy was devoted
to her new position on the executive committee of
Histadrut, the General Federation of Jewish Labor in
Palestine.

Almost 50 percent of all Jewish workers in the
country belonged to Histadrut. This unique labor
union not only set standards for the working conditions and wages of its workers but also built its own
factories. It owned a publishing house, a newspaper,
and several schools. Because of its participation in so
many areas of life, Histadrut was a powerful organization. As one of its top officials, Golda became a member of the inner circle of Jewish leadership.

Because her work took so much of her time and
energy, she and Morris saw less of each other. Realiz-

Golda and Morris Myerson with their
children, Sarah and Menahem

ing how much their interests and goals had grown apart, they both agreed that the time had come to separate. Golda kept the children in a small apartment in Tel Aviv while Morris remained in Haifa, where he had lived during the years that Golda and the children were in America.

Golda had little time for her children and she bitterly regretted this. She didn't like being away from Sarah and Menahem all day but her sense of duty and her desire to help Jews everywhere forced her to find work that would lead to a better future for her people.

Golda was also unhappy about parting from Morris. She said, "My husband was such a decent man . . . learned, kind, and good. . . . He taught me everything fine I know: music, poetry . . ." But soon she had little time to think of her own problems.

In 1939 World War II broke out. Hitler persecuted the Jews of every country his forces invaded. But now persecution led to extermination. With the war in progress, millions of Jews had little hope of escaping death. But Golda went to work with renewed energy. She said that from this point on "there is no Zionism save the rescue of the Jews."

"Somehow We Will Manage..."

While Golda was trying hard to find new ways to bring more Jews to Palestine, the British government was finding new ways to keep them out. During these years Great Britain was in control of Palestine. The British government wanted to remain friends with the Arabs so they could maintain their influence in the Middle East. But they could not do this unless they stopped Jewish immigration.

To accomplish this goal, the British issued a new

decree in 1939 called the White Paper. It reversed the policy of the 1917 Balfour Declaration, which supported the creation of a Jewish state. The White Paper limited Jewish immigration to a total of 100,000 over the next five-year period, after which it forbade any immigration at all.

Meanwhile, Golda knew that more and more Jews were being killed in Europe every day. Nothing was more important than saving their lives. But sometimes the people she was working with became discouraged. One day an old friend of Golda's said, "What is the good of trying to save lives? The British will allow only a few of the refugee ships to dock in Palestine."

"The British can't control *all* of the shipping," Golda said. "We will have the refugees come on little boats. They will land at night. The British patrols are too small to patrol the entire coastline every night!"

"Yes," said the friend, who was very depressed. "And then what will happen to these poor people?"

"We will take them to a kibbutz," Golda said. "We will hide them in apartments. Someway, somehow, we will manage to rescue as many Jews as we can. If we don't help, no one else will!"

Many of the refugees who were caught by the British were sent to camps on Cyprus, an island in the eastern Mediterranean. Here they lived in tents under very harsh conditions. Although relief agencies provided food, there was not very much to go around. The tents were cold and people had to huddle together for warmth.

After visiting one of these camps, Golda reported that she had found little children living there who had never seen a blade of grass. Others had never seen a wild flower. She was saddened to discover that they had no place to play but the muddy streets of the camp. Many children were sick.

Over and over again Golda went to the British. As the chief representative of all Jewish organizations in Palestine, she calmly but firmly told them that thousands of children would die if they remained in the camps. She insisted that the British permit the children to come to Palestine without their parents. And, as before, her great determination and willpower brought results. Finally the British agreed and the first shiploads of children began to arrive.

Meanwhile, the United States had entered the war in 1941. By 1944 the German armies were retreating. And finally, in the 1945, the Allies defeated Nazi Germany. Of the 25 million people who were killed in the war 6 million were Jewish. This was almost half the entire world population of Jewish people.

*Over-crowded ships brought desperate
refugees to Israel.*

The Jews were systematically slaughtered in the concentration camps that the Nazis had constructed throughout Europe. People everywhere grieved when the news of this hideous atrocity was released. Golda, of course, mourned for the loss of these innocent victims, who included 1 million children. But as usual she thought ahead to the work which must be done if the survivors were to be saved.

Her spirits began to rise when, in 1946, President Harry S Truman announced that the American government would support the creation of a Jewish state. What wonderful news! Now Golda knew that the reality of a Jewish homeland was closer than ever before.

But the American announcement did not change Britain's attitude toward Jewish immigration. Every week British soldiers continued to turn away ships carrying thousands of refugees. Since no other nation would accept these homeless people, the only places they could go were to centers called "displaced person camps" which had been established throughout Europe and on the island of Cyprus.

Finally the British decided that they would do a better job of keeping the Jews out of Palestine if they did not allow them to leave European ports. One of the ships they would not permit to sail was the *Fede,* at anchor in La Spezia harbor in Italy.

Golda said that all the refugees should go on a hunger strike. They should not eat, she suggested, until the British allowed the *Fede* to sail. Golda announced that she too would take no food until the ship was on its way to Palestine.

Her ceaseless efforts to bring about the creation of a Jewish state had made Golda's name well known. Her fast would draw attention to the plight of the refugees and would create bad publicity for the British.

The first day of her fast was the hardest. Golda was terribly hungry, especially at dinner time. But on the second day it didn't seem to matter so much. On the third day, Golda was so weak that she couldn't work. Her fast, and that of the others, was getting attention in the press throughout the world. The British did not want Golda to become a martyr. Finally, after the fast had gone on for 104 hours, they allowed the *Fede* to sail. Golda had to go to the hospital to recover but she said that it was a small price to pay.

For at last her years of struggling were beginning to bring results. On November 29, 1947—just one year after President Truman gave his support to the idea of a Jewish state—the General Assembly of the United Nations passed a resolution of the greatest importance.

It said that Palestine should be partitioned into two different countries. One would be an independent Jewish state, the other an independent Arab state. Jerusalem would become an international city.

At last the dream of centuries was becoming a reality! The wonderful news brought hope to Jewish people everywhere. For thousands of years they had wandered the earth looking for a home. Now, finally, that wandering might be ended. Golda also was filled with joy and thankfulness, but she knew that the Arab guns would be shooting before the sun rose the next day.

A Nation Is Reborn

Golda and other Jewish leaders knew that the Arabs would do anything to stop the establishment of a Jewish state. They had over 50,000 troops, heavy guns, armor, and an air force. The Jews had only a few thousand guns to use in their own defense.

"We have our backs against the wall," Golda told the Jewish people. "We don't even have a wall. We have a sea. The only friendly neighbor we have is the Mediterranean."

Golda was now a high official of the Jewish Agency, the governing body of the Jews in Palestine. She met constantly with other Jewish leaders to discuss the Arab threat. David Ben-Gurion, chief of the Jewish Agency, was very worried because the Jews had so few arms. Money was urgently needed to buy guns and ammunition. As before, it was decided that Golda should be sent to the United States to raise funds.

She arrived in New York on a cold day in January, 1948. Soon afterward she went to Chicago, where many Jewish-American groups were having a large meeting. When her turn came to speak, she did not use any notes. She never did. She spoke directly from her heart.

"I came for this very simple thing," she told her audience. " . . . I need twenty-five million dollars in a few weeks. . . . Every Jew in the country knows that within a few months a Jewish state in Palestine will be established. We have to pay for it. We know that the price we have to pay will be the lives of the best of our young people. But there is no doubt that the spirit of our young people will not falter. The spirit is there. But this spirit alone cannot face rifles and machine guns. . . . You cannot decide whether we fight or not. We will . . . nobody can change that. You can change only one thing . . . whether we shall be victorious. Yes, whether we fight or not—this is a decision we have to make. Whether we live or not—this is a decision *you* have to make."

When she finished speaking, many of the listening American Jews agreed to give Golda the money she needed. Grateful and pleased with her success, she went on to address other groups in America. She seized every opportunity to speak, stealing time only for a brief visit with her sister Clara, who had married and remained in the United States. Often she traveled by bus. She talked not only to the rich but to the poor as well. Listeners everywhere were impressed by Golda's simplicity, determination, and dedication. By the time she returned to Palestine she had raised over $50 million.

When David Ben-Gurion heard this, he said, "Someday when history will be written it will be said that there was a Jewish woman who got the money which made the State of Israel possible."

Quickly men were sent to Europe to purchase arms. Soon the huge crates were being unloaded from planes and ships. But whenever Golda talked to leaders of the Haganah they told her that they still had very few arms compared to the Arabs. The difference in the size of the opposing populations was also enormous. Whereas there were only 650,000 Jews at this time, the population of the hostile Arab countries numbered 40 million.

Violence was increasing every day. No one could be sure where the next Arab bomb would explode. Still, plans for the creation of the State of Israel continued. It was finally decided that statehood would be declared on May 14, 1948, at 4:00 P.M.

David Ben-Gurion called a special session of the Jewish National Council to meet in the Museum of Modern Art in Tel Aviv. One by one the Jewish leaders signed the Proclamation of Independence. Golda was one of two women who signed this historic paper.

Later she said, "After I signed, I cried. When I studied American history as a schoolgirl and I read about those who signed the Declaration of Independence, I couldn't imagine those were real people doing something real. And there I was sitting down and signing a declaration of independence."

There were great celebrations throughout the new nation. That is what the world called Israel—a new nation. But the Jews knew that it was not a new nation but a nation reborn. Many centuries had passed since A.D. 70, when the Jews were forced to leave Palestine, but they had never given up the dream of returning to their homeland. Golda summed up their feelings simply when she said, "We are not a new

On May 14, 1948, Golda was one of thirty-eight signers of Israel's Proclamation of Independence.

people. We are an old people that have come back to its old home."

Everywhere people danced in the streets. They sang. They laughed. They cried with happiness. Golda remained in Tel Aviv that night to meet with members of the Haganah. "The Arabs are massing at the border," they told her. "There is no doubt that they will cross tonight."

The following morning the Egyptians made their first air raid. Their armies attacked from the south while those of Syria and Jordan approached from the north and east. Soon Jerusalem was cut off from the rest of Israel.

There was little food left in the city. People were allowed only one piece of bread and four olives every day. They could have only one glass of water a day. Meanwhile, the members of the United Nations Security Council argued about what to do. Many nations that opposed the creation of a Jewish state opposed a cease-fire. Finally, because of the strong support of the United States, a cease-fire was ordered one month after the fighting had begun.

Golda watched the news with great concern, for once again she had left Israel to return to New York, where she hoped to raise more money for defense. While she was there, she received a cable from the

Israeli government. It asked if she would serve as ambassador to Moscow.

Golda accepted the new assignment. Before long she was on her way to Russia with Sarah, whose job was to be radio operator at the Israeli Embassy and Sarah's new husband, Zacharia, who would be a code expert. Menahem was studying music in America.

Soon after her arrival Golda ordered that the embassy be run as much like a kibbutz as possible. One of her assistants said, "But you are an ambassador. The other ambassadors will expect you to live like one."

Golda said, "That may be so, but while I am here the work of each person will be respected. *All* work is important. The cook and the chauffeur will eat at the table with me and the rest of the staff. Everybody will get the same amount of spending money. And that goes for me, too!"

When she had the time, Golda shopped for food and she also did some of the cooking. The embassy was run just the way she wanted it to be. But Golda did not enjoy her work as ambassador as much as some of her other jobs. As ambassador she had to attend many parties and give a great deal of time to social affairs. Golda believed she could be more useful in Israel.

Her chance came in 1949. During this year an armistice was signed between Israel and her neighbors. Because the Arabs were still opposed to the creation of a Jewish state, the Israelis knew it was only a temporary peace. Golda was well aware this was no time to rest from her labors. She knew that a real, lasting peace was still a long way off. Much work remained to be done in the land she loved so much.

Golda had been offered a challenging new job. She would soon be involved with the problems of workers —a subject that had always been of great concern to her. Her next assignment: minister of labor.

Years of Travel, Years of Work

As the first Israeli minister of labor, Golda found
huge problems waiting for her. But she was not worried about the work to be done. "Let's have more
problems of absorption of Jews," she said. "If any-
body knows in the first place what it means to be a
refugee and in the second place how to solve a refugee
problem, we are tops. After all, we are a refugee people."

Every day thousands of new Jewish immigrants

poured into Israel. Many who had survived the war in Europe did not want to return to their homes. Others who had lived in Africa or the Near East had endured centuries of oppression. They also wanted the chance of a new life in Israel.

During Golda's first two years as minister of labor, more than 685,000 people became new citizens, nearly doubling Israel's population. These new Israelis needed jobs and homes. It was Golda's job to see that they found them as quickly as possible.

The only shelters that Israel could offer the newcomers were tents. The simplest food was provided. Thousands of immigrants had to wait for months and sometimes years for better homes. But jobs came more quickly. Most new immigrants were sent to farms and villages as soon as possible. Many were given work in the orange groves. Others were kept busy building roads.

Golda worked sixteen hours a day every day of the week. But this was not a new routine for her, because she had always worked long hours. She was one of those lucky people whose work is also their pleasure. Giving poor families shelter and work gave *her* more pleasure than anything else could.

Every week she spent one full day visiting farms and immigrant villages. She talked to students who

*Immigrants who flocked to the new state
of Israel lived in tent camps while waiting
for new homes and jobs.*

were learning new crafts and visited new housing projects that were being constructed.

Sometimes the people in her office suggested that Golda slow down. They said she should not tire herself out by moving around so much. She answered, "You can't work in the office if you don't work in the field."

One of the problems created by the new immigrants could not be solved even by Golda. Thousands of new Israelis came from Egypt, Syria, India, North Africa, and many other non-European countries. For centuries they had lived in these places. Their speech, customs, and cultural background were different from those of the Jews who came from Europe. They were not skilled workers and most were very poor.

Soon problems began to grow between these Jews and those who had come from Europe. Golda knew that much time would have to pass before this problem could be solved. She was certain that vocational training and education would narrow the gap between the European Jews and those from other countries. Once in a while a European Jew would suggest that non-Europeans should not be allowed to enter Israel. Golda was firmly opposed to this. "*All* Jews will *always* be welcome in Israel," she said.

All her life she had worked for this goal. She would

Golda as minister of labor

not depart from it now. She agreed that the problems the immigrants faced were enormous, but she never stopped believing they were problems that human intelligence and hard work could solve. Because of this work, Israel had become fruitful. It would become even *more* fruitful. Golda told foreigners, "The only thing we have ever wanted to conquer is the desert. It is the only joy we have in conquest and we do something about it."

In 1957 Golda became Israel's foreign minister. And in her new job she would have a new name. David Ben-Gurion had urged her to change Myerson to its Hebrew form, which was Meir (pronounced May-EAR—"illuminate" in Hebrew).

One of Golda's major goals as foreign minister was to increase the aid being given to the developing nations. The Israelis had much valuable experience they could share with other countries faced with similar problems.

Many of these countries in Africa and Asia had only recently won their independence. Golda believed that the people of these lands, like the Jews, had long been oppressed peoples. She felt an obligation to help them as much as she could. As a good politician she also knew that Israel must make as many friends as possible.

67

Because Israel's problems were so much like those of the African nations, the Israelis could be especially helpful to these countries. Many of these nations did not know how to irrigate their desert lands or how to increase food production. Israel sent her experts to help them. Many Israelis were also highly skilled physicians and scientists. Several of these experts, as well as those in other fields, went to Africa to work and to teach.

Golda began her own trips to Africa in February, 1958, when she visited Ghana, Nigeria, and the Ivory Coast. Everywhere she was received with great warmth. In Nigeria an official said to her, "Your Foreign Ministry is mislabeled 'foreign.' To us it is a Friendly Ministry."

Israeli experts did not only advise and teach. They rolled up their sleeves and went to work with the Africans. This surprised many Africans. One told Golda with amazement, "For the first time I've seen a white man work with his hands."

Golda sometimes grew sad when she thought that the Jews and Arabs could not also help each other. Once she said, "Israel has sent thousands of men and women to other continents to bring to the people the results of our experience, to work with them as brothers, to help them in their development plans. It will

*Prime Minister Kenyatta welcomes Israeli
foreign minister Golda Meir to Kenya.*

be a great day when we don't have to travel thousands of miles . . . and the young Jew from this side of the Jordan on his farm will cross the Jordan, not with tanks, not with planes, but with tractors and with the hand of friendship as between a farmer and farmer, as between a human being and human being. A dream? I am sure it will come true."

Golda had worked tirelessly to make this dream come a little nearer to fulfillment. She was sixty-six in 1964 and wondering if the time had come to retire. She wanted to see more of her children and grandchildren. They did not know their grandfather, for Morris had died years before in 1951.

Menahem, now thirty, was a concert cellist. When not traveling, he lived in Tel Aviv with his wife and three children. Sarah, Golda's daughter, lived with her husband and three children in a kibbutz. It would be nice, Golda thought, to visit them more often. She could also see more of Shana, who with her children and grandchildren had remained in Israel. Clara, who had chosen to live in the United States, tried to visit her sisters in Israel once a year. Perhaps this year Golda could spend more time with her younger sister during the few weeks they could be together.

Golda's time had always been limited. She had never taken a vacation. Once one of the men who worked closely with her suggested that it was time she did.

"Why?" she asked. "Do you think I'm tired?"

"No," he said, "but I am."

"So *you* take a vacation," Golda said firmly.

But now she admitted that she, too, was growing tired. In 1966 she reluctantly came to the decision that the time had come for her to retire.

Golda Meir, Prime Minister

The first months of Golda's retirement were a great
pleasure. She read widely. She visited old friends and
spent much more time with her family. And yet she
was not as happy as she had been before her retirement.

One day a former coworker came to see her. "Are
you enjoying your free time?" he asked.

"Yes," Golda said, "but ..."

"But what?" the man asked with interest.

"I need something to do," Golda confessed. "All of my life I have worked. I can't be happy unless I am doing something useful."

"I knew that was happening," said the friend. "It's the reason I came to see you."

Golda's friend offered her a job as leader of the Mapai—the biggest labor party in Israel. She accepted at once and began work eagerly. It was good to go to the office again every morning. And she liked the challenge of the new work. The problems of labor had always been of great interest to Golda. She wished she could give her job *all* her attention. However, this she could not do, for once again, in 1967, Israel was in great danger.

Every day Arab guerrillas were committing new acts of terror. They threw bombs into crowded buses and into market places where women were shopping for food. Every week Israelis were being killed or injured by these acts of terrorism. Radio Cairo often broadcast, "The Arab people are firmly resolved to wipe Israel off the map. . . ."

Although she was not a part of the government, Golda was told what was happening. She was informed that the Arabs were preparing for a new war. Russia was sending the Arabs thousands of tons of war equipment. Golda was asked for advice.

She knew the problems that Israel must face. There were 40 million Arabs but only 2.5 million Israelis. The Arabs were rich. The Israelis were poor. The Arabs were fighting for what they believed was their land. But the Israelis were fighting for their lives. They knew they must be victorious or be destroyed.

Golda said, "Our neighbors want to see us dead. This is not a question that leaves much room for compromise...."

When she met with high government and army officials, she said, "I don't see how war can be avoided. Nobody is going to help us. But I'm convinced we'll win."

The Israeli government came to the conclusion that it must strike first. The Arabs were sure to attack, but if the Israelis waited for that attack, they would be put on the defensive and have far less chance of success. Their very survival depended upon their ability to fight a quick, victorious war because they did not have the reserve power of the Arabs. Finally, plans were made for the attack to begin on the morning of June 5, 1967.

In only six days of war, Israel drove Egypt out of the Sinai desert. Israeli troops occupied the Golan Heights in Syria and the Jordan River's West Bank. Jerusalem

*An Israeli tank-column advances across the
desert during the Six Day War.*

was reunited. Afterward the battles of this period were called "The Six Day War."

The Israelis did not want the occupied lands. They believed they *must* have them to protect themselves from new Arab attacks. It was only a question of time until the Arabs rearmed and threatened once again to wipe Israel off the map.

Although there had been a great Israeli victory, Golda said sadly, "We don't want wars even when we win. The Israelis have no joy in killing, no joy in shooting, no joy in winning wars. The Israeli soldiers were the saddest victorious army in history."

Again peace came to Israel. The people looked forward to building new industries and to enlarging their farms and orchards. Golda finished her work as leader of the Mapai. Once again she was spending her days reading, visiting friends or family. She was now seventy years old and slowing down.

Some people thought she could no longer be of use to the government. They said, "Golda is a sick woman. She is too old for any important job." But Golda's party—the Mapai—did not think she was too old. In 1968, after they won the elections and the right to name a new prime minister, they asked Golda to become head of the government.

There was much talk about her age. Golda said

After the reunification of Jerusalem,
Golda visited the historic Wailing Wall.

simply, "Being seventy is not a sin. It is not a joy either." Her long experience had prepared her well for the job of prime minister. She was strong and could work long hours. Never before had she taken a job that offered so many challenges. But the government believed in her. The Israeli people believed in her.

Golda did not waste time or words. She started work at once.

A Life for Israel

As prime minister of Israel, Golda had greater responsibilities than ever before. Her first job was to form a new cabinet. An excellent administrator, she chose her new ministers with great care. She had known most of the men or had worked with them for several years. Many had a lot of experience but few had as much as Golda.

Fifty years had passed since she arrived in the dry land then called Palestine. Vast changes had taken place during that time. The kibbutzim were now green and flourishing. Golda recalled that "At the beginning Merhavia offered nothing but swamps and sand, but soon it became a garden full of orange trees, and only looking at it gave me such joy that I could have spent my whole life there."

Israel's economy had grown quickly also and there was now full employment. Many small industries had developed, and Israel produced almost all the food it needed. There was so much citrus fruit that large quantities were exported. And the number of Israelis had grown to almost 3 million—a good-sized population for a country about the size of New Jersey.

And yet, much work remained to be done. The job of prime minister made great demands on Golda. The occupied lands created new problems. Many Arabs were now under Israeli rule for the first time and most of them were extremely poor people. Their villages did not have sewers, plumbing, or electricity.

Speaking of these Arabs, Golda said, "We have to do everything we possibly can, whether it is in economic development, certainly in employment, in social services, in every way, to see that these people are taken care of."

Gradually this vital work was undertaken. Many Arabs were surprised to discover that their standard

Many years of work transformed
Merhavia into an oasis.

of living was higher under the Israelis than it had been under their own government. Their health improved. Their incomes grew larger. Much had been accomplished when suddenly, on October 4, 1973, a grave new threat came to Israel.

When the alarms sounded, thousands of people were in the temples. The Arabs chose to attack on the holiest day of the year—Yom Kippur. When people heard the air raid sirens screaming, they rushed into the streets. Everywhere radios were blaring the news: The Arab armies were attacking on all frontiers.

The Israelis were confused. They could not believe that the Arabs had chosen Yom Kippur on which to attack. Israel was not prepared for war. During the first grim days the Arab armies moved quickly. Israeli soldiers tried to hold them back while the country mobilized.

Every able-bodied man and woman worked to save the country from destruction. Since military service is compulsory for Israeli women, they shared the responsibility of defending their country. Golda put most of her regular work aside and gave all her attention to the war effort. Her work day became even longer than before.

Lou Kaddar, her assistant, said, "Golda can do without rest for a long time if she has to . . . then when she has the chance, she'll sleep fourteen hours to make up for it." Now her beloved Israel was in danger and she could not rest until that danger had passed. Mrs. Kaddar added, "When she's challenged, all her spirits are awake . . . it's in her character to be optimistic."

The United States was the only country in the world that came to Israel's aid. Troops were not sent but massive supplies of war matériel were flown in. With the help of these supplies the Israelis were able to stop the advance of the Arab armies, which were being given military aid by the Russians. Israel now had time to prepare a counteroffensive.

Golda met daily with Moshe Dayan, the minister of defense. They discussed different ways to stop the Arabs. Finally, she approved Dayan's brilliant plan of attack and watched with pride as the Israeli armies gradually began to push back the Arabs.

Meanwhile, the United States was working hard to bring about a cease-fire. Golda flew to the United States to meet with President Nixon in Washington, D.C. She also discussed peace moves with Dr. Henry Kissinger, the secretary of state, when he came to Israel. After much bloodshed the cease-fire went into effect on October 24, 1973.

In December the Israelis and Arabs joined each other at a peace conference in Geneva, Switzerland.

*Prime Minister Golda Meir confers
with Moshe Dayan, the minister of defense.*

In the twenty-five years since the creation of Israel, this was the first meeting between the two peoples.

The first problem to be resolved was the establishment of cease-fire lines. After many months of discussion these were agreed upon. But meanwhile, Palestinian guerrilla raids continued to take Israeli lives. The tension and bitterness caused by the sudden destructive war and by the continuing attacks created many problems within the country. Thousands of Israeli soldiers and civilians had been killed or wounded.

Many Israelis blamed the government. They said poor planning and inadequate intelligence had left the country vulnerable to a surprise attack. There were calls for a change of government, for new leadership.

Golda had wanted to retire even before the war began, but while it was in progress she could not leave her post. The months of emotional tension and long hours of work had taken a heavy toll on her strength. She seemed to have aged years within a few months and she was weary. She had served her country long and well but now she knew that the time had come for her political life to end. In April 1974 she announced that she would retire and that nothing would change her mind. Golda remained head of the government until June 3, 1974, when Yitzhak Rabin, a native-born Israeli, or *sabra,* took over the responsibilities of prime minister.

From now on, Golda would watch from the sidelines as negotiations toward a permanent peace continued. She knew that it would be extremely difficult to achieve a lasting peace, yet she was convinced that peace eventually must come to the Middle East. Perhaps the young Israelis would find the way.

Golda said of them fondly, "This is a wonderful generation—straight, fearless, beautiful, capable—there isn't a thing they can't do." Many of these young people were now seeking a louder voice in politics. Golda hoped that more women would enter this important field.

During the course of her long career she had become convinced that women must be encouraged to take active roles in society. "In my opinion," she said, "women can be good rulers, good leaders . . . women are more practical, more realistic." She had shown Israel and the world that a woman could be practical. She had shown both Israel and the world that a woman could be realistic. She had proved that a woman could help build a nation and also lead it with intelligence and courage.

Golda never doubted that one day the Arabs and Israelis would live as peaceful neighbors. Each group

Golda Meir, strong, dedicated and compassionate

had much to teach the other. Both could work to-gether to create a new and better life for the people of the Middle East.

Of this future time Golda said, "I'm convinced that some day—I don't know when—someone—and I envy him already—will stand before the communities of the world with the message that there is peace in Israel—joy in Israel—and only joy in Israel. And we will know that everything which contributed to that day was worthwhile."

Certainly no one worked harder for that day than Golda Meir.

Chronology

1898   On May 3, Golda Mabowitz is born in Kiev, Russia.

1906   The Mabowitz family emigrates to America and settles in Milwaukee, Wisconsin.

1916   Golda graduates from high school.

1917   Great Britain issues the Balfour Declaration on November 2.

On December 24, Golda Mabowitz is married to Morris Myerson in Milwaukee.

1921 The Myersons sail to Palestine on the S.S. *Pocahontas* and arrive at Tel Aviv on July 14. That fall they are accepted as new members of the Merhavia kibbutz.

1924 The Myersons leave Merhavia and move to Jerusalem where a son, Menahem, is born.

1926 The Myersons' daughter, Sarah, is born.

1928 Golda becomes secretary of Moatzot Poalot, the Women's Labor Council.

1929 The Jewish Agency is created to represent the Palestinian Jews in their relationship with the British Mandatory Government.

1932 Golda takes Sarah to Beth Israel Hospital in New York for treatment of a kidney ailment; Golda meanwhile travels around the United States raising funds for the Pioneer Women.

1934 Golda is made a member of the executive committee of Histadrut, the Zionist labor union.

1938 Golda attends the International Conference on Refugees at Evian-les-Bains, France, as the Jewish observer from Palestine.

1939 On May 17, Great Britain issues the White Paper, reversing the goals of the Balfour Declaration.

World War II begins in September.

1940 Golda works for Haganah, the underground army.

1946 Golda becomes unofficial representative of all Jewish organizations in Palestine; she participates in the voluntary fast to save Jewish refugees on the *Fede*.

1947 On November 29, the United Nations votes for the creation of a new Jewish state.

1948 The State of Israel is proclaimed on May 14 and Golda signs the Proclamation of Independence; on June 7, she is appointed Israel's first ambassador to Russia.

1949 Israel signs armistice with Arab countries on February 24.

On April 20, Golda becomes Minister of Labor and Development.

1956 Golda Meir is appointed Foreign Minister.

1967 On June 5, Israel begins the Six-Day War.

1969 In February, Golda becomes Prime Minister of Israel.

1973 Israel is attacked by her Arab neighbors in the Yom Kippur War.

1974 In April, Golda Meir announces her retirement.

Bibliography

Agress, Eliyahu, *Golda Meir: Portrait of a Prime Minister.*
New York, Sabra Books, 1969

Eban, Abba, *My People: The Story of the Jews.* New
York, Random House, 1968

Levin, Meyer, *The Story of Israel.* New York, G. P. Putnam's Sons, 1966

Mann, Peggy, *Golda: The Story of Israel's Prime Minister.* New York, Coward, McCann & Geoghegan, Inc.,
1971

Meir, Golda, *This Is Our Strength* (edited by Henry M. Christman). New York, Macmillan, 1962

Syrkin, Marie, *Golda Meir: A Nation's Leader*. New York, G. P. Putnam's Sons, 1969

Fallaci, Oriana, "Golda Meir: On Being a Woman." *Ms.* Magazine, New York, April 1973

Photographs appear courtesy of:
Clara Stern: 11, 27, 45
Wide World Photos: 84
Zionist Archives: frontispiece, 8, 16, 33,
    50, 58, 64, 66, 69, 75, 77, 81, 87

Index

About the Author

A native of Omaha, Nebraska, Arnold Dobrin studied at the Chouinard Art Institute in Los Angeles, at the University of California at Los Angeles, and at the Academy de la Grande Chaumière in Paris. He lived in Rome for two years and has traveled extensively in Europe, Asia, and the Near East.

Mr. Dobrin is the author of many books for young readers, including *Aaron Copland; Igor Stravinsky;* and *Voices of Joy, Voices of Freedom.* He lives in Westport, Connecticut.